A Chronology of the Bible

*A Brief History of the Development of the Old and New
Testaments from their African and Asian Origins
to their European and European-American Revisions,
Versions, etc.*

Yosef ben-Jochannan

Black Classic Press

A Chronology of the Bible

Printed by BCP Digital Printing, *a division of Black Classic Press*

Founded in 1978, Black Classic Press specializes in bringing
to light obscure and significant works by and about people
of African descent. If our books are not available in your
area, ask your local bookseller to order them. Our current
list of titles can be obtained by writing:

**Black Classic Press
c/o List
P.O. Box 13414
Baltimore, MD 21203-3414**

A Young Press With Some Very Old Ideas

Dedicated to truth, yet always mindful that

All faith is *False,* all faith is *True*
Truth is the shattered mirrors strewn
In myriad bits; while each *Believes*
his *Little Bit* the whole to own.

From: *The Kasidah of Haji Abu el-Yezdi;*
as translated by Sir Richard F. Burton

On the morning of Wednesday, July 11, 1973 in Chock Full O'Nuts Restaurant, Lenox Avenue and 135th Street, Harlem, New York City, New York, it was my very good fortune to be sitting for another fruitful session of *common ecumenical* talk among the following Black clergymen: Reverend George H. Polk of the Memorial Baptist Church, Reverend William F. Hawkins of the Metropolitan African Methodist Episcopal Church, Reverend Hawkins J. Plummer of the Salvation Baptist Church, and Reverend James Gunther of Transfiguration Lutheran Church, who joined us later on. Along with us were a few of our many lay friends. In the course of the conversation of the morning,(which centered around the last two volumes of *The Black Man's Religion,* a three-volume work that I am completing for publication later this year*), Reverend Polk suggested that:

> It would be of extreme importance that the average parishioner have some kind of understanding of the chronological development and order in which the King James *authorized* Version of The Old and New Testaments came about. . ., etc.

Reverend Hawkins and Reverend Plummer immediately supported the idea. It was then agreed that pages 82 through 86 of *The Need for a Black Bible,* (volume III of the above work), would be extracted as it were, then made into a lay people's pamphlet. And, that it would include a

---

*Publisher's Note—These three volumes were completed and published as *The Black Man's Religion: (* vol. I, *The African Origins of the Major Western Religions,* vol. II, *The Myth of Genesis and Exodus, and their Exclusion of their African Origins,* and vol. III, *The Need for a Black Bible). Volume I is now available; vols. II and III are currently scheduled for republication.*

few single paragraph comments on the subject of the origin and development of The Old and New Testaments by a few members of the Black clergy. The following is the result of that glorious communion we were all privileged to have had that heavenly morning.

As we look back into the history of the Holy Bible, or *holy scriptures as written by God-inspired scribes,* we seem to forget that all of the Bibles we use were the works of various writers, both men and women; but mostly men. And, that all of these works or books were compiled into what is today our various versions of "Holy Bibles" or "Holy Scrolls." We have also failed to realize that the Bibles we use today are the result of a period of hundreds of revisions and translations that cover approximately 2,495 years—from ca. 700 B. C. (BCE) to 1973 A. D.(CE).

Yet all in this period were preceded by much more earlier fundamentals created and developed by indigenous African people. These later on became the basic teachings of Judaism, and then Christianity. For even Moses, the father of The Old Testament, was an African who used much of the ancient teachings of his fellow Africans of the Nile River (Blue And White) and Great Lakes regions Mysteries System of Northeast and Central-East Africa he allegedly passed down to other African Jews that converted them into what later became the Pentateuch or The Old Testament (Five Books of Moses or Holy Torah).

The very first "Bible" or "Scroll" on record produced by man, with regards to paying honor and divine respect to a "Creator of all mankind," was that of the African people of the Nile Valley and Great Lakes regions of Central, East and Northeast Africa.

They were no different than the Africans we see today in the Harlems and Timbuctoos of the entire world we erroneously call: "Negroes," "Colored folks," and "Black people" today. It was called by its African creator and developers, The Book of the Coming Forth by Day and by Night. It was translated from its original hieroglyphic text into the English language by many Europeans since the latter part of the nineteenth century A.D. The easiest one to read is called, *The (Egyptian) Book of the Dead.*

This translation was done by Sir Ernest A. Wallis Budge, and published in London, England during the year 1895 A.D.

Since the original Bible was produced by the African approximately 3,400 years before The Old Testament, and more than 4,200 years before The New Testament, countless versions of it have been written and published. From this base, all of the Biblical references in this pamphlet are rendered. You will notice that they follow in sequential order. . . the two originals and all of the versions of The Old and New Testaments. For further details beyond this pamphlet you should read Volume III of *The Black Man's Religion.*

Although it is the King James (authorized) Version of The Old and New Testaments that most Protestant Christians use as *"the one, and only, true Bible,"* you *must* be reminded that it is one of the very late of the many versions of the Bible, and that many of the other versions that preceded it are easier to read, which includes most of the other English language versions since its publication in 1611 A.D. You will also notice that there were many English versions before the King James (authorized) Version of The Old and New Testaments. Its popularity was due to the fact that the rulers of Great Britain's military power were able to force practically everyone in their hundreds of colonies throughout the entire world to adopt the *official Bible of the church of England as the one, and only, true Holy Bible.*

It will prove most beneficial for Bible study classes to make comparisons between the various versions. This method of study will not only enrich your retention of the teachings in the Bible, but it will also give you a better understanding of the role the African people commanded in the founding of Judaism and Christianity. You will equally understand that most Blacks do not know that The Old and New Testaments historically, geographically, sociopolitically, racially, etc. are *part and parcel of their own heritage.* Some of the major versions, and the two original Bibles follow in chronological order below along with highlights of the historical events that caused and/or influenced them. I have shown the map below as an aid to the Land of the Bible (Africa and Asia; followed very much later by Europe).

Archaeological Sites of Ta-Merry and Ta-Nehisi 3200 to 47 or 30 B.C.E.

1. Memphis, early capital of Ta-Merry during Aha's reign—founder of the First Dynasty, c. 3200 B.C.E.

2. On, or Heliopolis, where African astronomers made man's first calendar, c. 4100 B.C.E.

3. Sakhara, or Saqqara, home of first Step Pyramid, built by architect Imhotep for Pharaoh Djoser, III, of the Third Dynasty, c. 2780 B.C.E. The true beginning of the Pyramid Age—the Old Kingdom period.

4. Ghizeh, or Giza, home of the largest of the pyramids. These pyramids were built during the Fourth and Fifth Dynasties, c.2680-2270 B.C.E.

A Chronological List
of the Original Book of the Dead,
Old Testament, New Testament, and Qur'an, etc.

10,000 - 6000 B.C.E.(B.C.)

Stellar Calendar in use by the ancient Nile Valley Africans and other Africans of the Great Lakes regions.

4000 - 4000

Solar Calendar in use by the ancient Nile Valley Africans. The Book of the Coming Forth by Day and by Night was introduced in its revised state, also known today as *The Book of the Dead* (as translated from hieroglyph to English by Sir Ernest A. Wallis Budge, London, England, 1885 C.E.).

3760

Beginning of the "World"(Creation Story according to the Hebrews' adaptation of Moses' Pentateuch much later on).

3100 (4100)

Dynastic periods begin under the Nubian named Aha or Narmer whom Herodotus called "Menes"; end of the Pre-dynastic Old Kingdoms.

1770

Birth of Abraham—the first Hebrew (Jew)—in Asia, at the City of Ur, Chaldea during its colonial period under African rule to Sun Worshipers (parents).

1675

First foreign invasion of Alkebu-lan (Africa). Egypt overrun by Hyksos invaders from the banks of the Oxus River around the so-called "Fertile Crescent." These were the first of the so-called "Semitic Peoples" in Africa.

1670
Abraham and his family arrived in Africa (Qamt, which the Hebrews are to later rename Mizrain, today's Moslem's Mizrair, and Christian's Egypt). Famine and disease drove the handful of Hebrew shepherds into Africa.

1320 (?)
Moses (an African of Qamt) born in Africa. The supposed "Father Of The Old Testament".

1230 (?)
Moses' civil war against Pharaoh Rameses II. Date of the "Exodus of the Hebrews" from Succoth to Mount Sinai. (Central Qamt, or Egypt, to Eastern Qamt).

1190 (?)
Date of Moses' disappearance (*death*).

700-500
Pentateuch (Five Books of Moses, Holy Torah, or The Old Testament) completed and placed into circulation. A version of The Book of the Coming Forth by Day and by Night, as distorted by Hebrews living in "Egypt"; supposedly "the ...words of God passed on to Moses..., " who allegedly "...passed them on, word for word, to God-inspired scribes...," etc.

250-100
Septuagint Version of the Pentateuch. The first Greek Version of the Hebrew's distortion of The Book of the Coming Forth by Day and by Night written by seventy-two writers: rabbis and other "scholars" ("God-inspired scribes" according to the teachings of the Jews, Christians and Moslems). This was written at Alexandria, Egypt (North Africa) by African Hebrews. It was a compilation of forty-five books, also called the Alexandrian Canon. This version was used by the earliest Greek and Latin Church.

30-4 (?)

Birth of Jesus Christ of Nazareth. Announcement of a Hebrew boy born of Hebrew (Israelite) parents named Joseph and Mary.

12 C.E. (A.D.)

Jesus Christ challenges his teachers (rabbis) in the temple at Jerusalem. Jesus sent to Africa to hide from Roman Emperor Herod, to study in the lodges, and for his initiation in the Mysteries System of Egypt–North Africa.

33

Jesus Christ murdered by Romans and Jews.

52-100

Koine Bible Version. First Christian New Testament Bible published and circulated. Written in the Greek language. Parts were written in "Aramaic"; allegedly the "language Jesus Christ spoke among the common people of Israel. . ., " etc., called the Palestinian Canon Version. This text was developed by the Synod of Jamnia as a version of the Pentateuch.

322

Council of Bishops at Nicene. This group of Bishops of the Roman Catholic Church met upon an edict of Emperor Constantine to take action on the books of the Bible, along with Mary's "Immaculate Conception" and "Virgin Birth of Jesus Christ."

323

Bishops of Nicene on majority vote approved the "Immaculate Conception" and "Virgin Birth of Jesus Christ" to Mary. Jesus Christ declared to be "God"—"The Father, The Son, and Holy Ghost" (today's Spirit).

350-400

New Testament Canon Version. The first twenty-seven books. A revision of the original total of forty-five books.

400
Saint Jerome's Latin Vulgate Version. Based upon the Greek Septuagint Version.

550
European Version of Babylonian Talmud. Publication of the Sixth century C.E. racist version of the interpretation of the Pentateuch by European rabbis and other "scholars."

570 (B.H. 52)
Birth of Prophet Mohamet ibn Abdullah. Historians argue as to whether he was born at Mecca or Medina. (B.H. means before the Hejira).

622
Mohamet ibn Abdullah flees Mecca; establishment of the religion of Islam at the oasis of Yathrib outside of Medina; the year of the Hejira (A. H.).

670 (?)
Holy Qur'an (English Koran) compiled and circulated. This Moslem Bible adopted the basic teachings of The Old Testament and The New Testament. Serious modifications to the teachings in both were made to the satisfaction of the Prophet and his followers—the chief one of whom was the writer of the first section, "Bilal," an African from Ethiopia, East Africa.

600 - 900
Masoretic Text. This version was written in Hebrew by Jewish scribes of the Masorite school. This version is the basic one most so-called "Orthodox Christians" still refer to as the original source, which is incorrect. It was, in fact, the basic Bible used for many more translations into various languages for many generations of Christians.

1382
John Wycliff's first complete English Version of The Old and New Testaments.

1460 (?)

Moses ben Maimonides Talmud. "Official translation" of Five Books of Moses according to Moses ben Maimonides of Spain, et al.

1456

Gutenberg Version of the Holy Bible. The "first book" ever printed by typesetting method. A folio-type edition of the Latin Vulgate Version. It was not *the first book*, as so many Christians believe.

1516

Saint Erasmus Version of the Holy Bible. This was written in the Greek language.

1529

Reverend Martin Luther protests against the "Edict of The Diet of Worms" against the Reformation. Birth of the major revolution in the Roman Catholic Church and the formation of the foundation of Protestantism.

1535

William Tyndale Version—written in English. The "first English" language version used for further translations, etc. in English.

1535

Miles Coverdale Version of the Holy Bible. Written in English as a tribute to King Henry VIII of Great Britain.

1537

The first Bible ever printed in England.

1537

Saint Matthew Version of the Holy Bible. Written in English according to the Coverdale and Tyndale Versions.

1539
Coverdale Great Bible Version. An amalgamation of the Coverdale and Tyndale Bibles, as authorized by the monarch of Great Britain—Henry VIII.

1560
Geneva Version of the Holy Bible. Written by Coverdale, William Whittingham, John Knox, et al. Produced in Geneva, Switzerland. The "first English version with chapters divided into verses." Done during the reign of Queen Mary of Great Britain, and in her honor.

1582 - 1610
Douay-Rheims Version of the Holy Bible. Written by scholars of the Roman Catholic Church. An English translation of the Latin Vulgate Version at the Catholic College. The name was due to The New Testament issuance at Rheims in 1582 C.E.; whereas The Old Testament issuance was at Douay, France in ca. 1609 or 1610 C. E.

1611
King James Authorized Version of The Old and New Testaments. Written by subjects of King James of Great Britain to satisfy conditions set down by himself and the royalty of his realm, all of which were opposed by the Pope in Rome, particularly those aspects that allowed James to maintain his own polygamous behavior. This is the Bible most Black people believe to be "the one and only true Holy Scripture. . . the actual words of God" (meaning Jesus Christ of Nazareth), which was allegedly ". . .written by God-inspired scribes." The Black clergy and Black theologians perpetuate this myth in order to continue their manipulation of their fellow African (Black) people who so believe.

1885
English Revised Version of the Holy Bible. A revision of the King James Authorized Version of The Old and New Testaments by Europeans and European-Americans from the United States of America. This was the "first

time in history" that European-Americans were allowed to participate in the further distortions of the original teachings from the Africans and Asians of the Nile Valley and Tigris-Euphrates valleys.

1901
American Standard Version of the Holy Bible. By the American Committee that worked on the English Revised Version of 1885 C. E. Jealousy between Europeans and European-Americans caused the production of this version.

1924
The Moffatt Version of the Holy Bible. By James Moffatt. Written in twentieth century "modern" English.

1931
Smith-Goodspeed Version of the Holy Bible. The Old Testament prepared by J. M. Powis-Smith as editor; The New Testament by Edgar J. Goodspeed of the University of Chicago.

1941
The Confraternity Version of the Holy Bible. A revision of the Douay-Rheims-Challomer Version. The New Testament section was published by the Episcopal Confraternity of the Christian Doctrine of the Roman Catholic Church; The Old Testament section remained according to the Latin Vulgate Version.

1945-1949
Knox Version of the Holy Bible. Written in English by Msgr. Ronald A. Knox according to the Latin Vulgate Version; authorized by the Roman Catholic Command of Wales and England to counteract the King James Version.

1952
Revised Standard Version of the Holy Bible. Written by a group of the United States of America's European-American "God-inspired scribes" under the sponsorship of the National Council Of Churches Of Christ.

1961
New English Version of the Holy Bible. Written by a group of English writers under the sponsorship of the Protestant Churches of Britain, and by others from Oxford and Cambridge University Presses.

1973
The Common American Language Version. This was approved by a group of rabbis, priests, ministers, and theologians who found all of its contents satisfactory to the teachings of Judaism and Christianity in the United States of America.

Most Jewish, Christian and Moslem parishioners do not know very much about the basic book they use as their only religious and divine guide. The reason for this is based in fact that very few of them, not unlike yourself, know the answer to the following questions related to the history and development of the original Bibles and their many versions.

Questions and Answers

Q. What is meant by the word Bible?

A. Bible (Latin - BIBLIA; Greek - BIBLIA; a noun) - a collection of writings, little book; any collection or book of writings sacred to a particular religion; a book regarded as the only authoritative one in its class, such as the Christian New Testament, Jewish Old Testament, and Moslem Qur'an, etc.

Q. When was the first Bible written?

A. Approximately 5000 to 4100 B. C. (B. C. E. or Before Christ). It was written in Ta-Merry (Qamt, Kimit, Sais, etc.)—the African nation the Israelites renamed Mizrain, and the English translated into Egypt.

Q. When was the first Hebrew (or Jewish) Bible written?

A. Between the years 700 and 500 B. C. by Egyptian Hebrews Jews) of Egypt.

Q. When was the first Christian Bible written?

A. Approximately from 52 to 100 After the Death of Christ (A.D. or C.E.).

Q. How many books were in the first Jewish Bible?

A. Four. These were expanded into five at the Council of Jamnia.

Q. How many books were in the first Christian Bible?

A. Forty-five. They were reduced to 27 at the Nicene Conference.

Q. Which one of the Bibles is called The Old Testament?

A. The Five Books of Moses or Pentateuch, also known as the Holy Torah.

Q. Who was the African that introduced the story about "Creation of the World"; when was he born, and what was the name of the Pharaoh he fought?

A. Moses (drawn from water); born in Egypt, North Africa; who fought Pharaoh Rameses II who reigned over Egypt from ca. 1298 to 1232 B.C.(or B.C.E.).

Q. What is the name of the original (first) Christian Bible, and in what language was it written?

A. Koine Bible: originally written in the Greek language and Aramaic (the language allegedly "spoken by Jesus Christ"—the "language of the people").

Q. Which Bible was "written in the language Christ spoke"?

A. See the answer given above. Also see my note for the period 52-100 A.D.

Q. Who is the main character in The Old Testament, and in The New Testament?

A. Ywh, also called "Jehovah, Adanoi, Adoni, Adonis, God, Father," etc. in The Old Testament; Jesus of Nazareth, also called "Jesus Christ, Joshua the Anointed, Lamb of God, Holy Ghost (Spirit), Savior, Redeemer,

Son, God, Trinity, Divine Spirit, Light of the World" in the New Testament.

Q. In what year was the Moslem (Muslim) Qur'an (or Bible) written?

A. Approximately in the year 670 A.D., or 48 A.H. (48 years following the founding of the Moslem religion, Islam, by Mohamet ibn Abdullah. A. H. means "After the Hejira"—the year Mohamet had to flee Mecca to save his life).

Q. How many versions of the Bible preceded the King James Version?

A. Sixteen major versions. There were many that failed to receive acclaim.

Q. Name at least one Bible written for another English monarch?

A. The Miles Coverdale Version written for King Henry VIII in 1535 A.D.

Q. What is the meaning of the word "version," and how does it differ from the following words: original and facsimile?

A. A translation of the Bible giving an account of one point of view. The original is the first base from which the version is taken. A facsimile is a direct copy of the original without any changes whatsoever.

Q. What is the difference between the Latin Vulgate and King James Versions?

A. Versions; usage of words; meaning of words; period of time; difference in belief about "the teachings of Jesus Christ", etc.

Q. Were all of the men who wrote all of the versions equally "inspired"?

A. It must be assumed that all of the writers were "inspired by God" if any of the versions from which the King James' is taken is correct. If any of the base versions is faulty, so must those taken from it follow in the same way.

Q. Would you accept another English version, and why?

A. Yes. Because the grammar and style would be easier to read and understand than the archaic Old English in which the King James Version is written.

Q. Who is the main character in all of the holy books of the world?

A. God. Whether He, She or It, all of the religions of the world recognize a divine entity that is translated into the English language meaning "God."

Q. Which was the original form of the Bible: book or scroll?

A. Scroll. The first was made from the papyrus plant of the Nile Valley.

Comments from the Clergy

The advent of the "Cultural Revolution" that swept the Black communities of the entire world also swept the religious conscience of the Black clergy. As leaders of the largest segment of the Black communities, the Black clergy generally suffer equally as much as their followers; thus it must equally deal with the proper information needed for an informed Black community, particularly in the area of the religious life. The first step must be with the human life style the history of religion teaches. In order to accomplish this end, the need to understand the main document of said teaching, its origin, its development, and its meaning, becomes the responsibility of the Black theologians, Black clergy, and the Black teachers. In this respect, the following members of the Black clergy comment on *A Chronology of the Bible.*

Rev. George P. Polk

This Bible chronology is a must for any serious student of God's sacred truth. Every Black Christian ought to know from whence his religion came. Dr. ben-Jochannan has accomplished this task admirably.

Rev. William F. Hawkins

When God summons a man for a specific task, the man is God-equipped for it. An accurate chronology of the Bible, written in easy reading style as set forth by Dr. ben-Jochannan, makes it easy for the Black clergy and Black teachers alike to better understand the Bible as a whole. I am proud to have the honor of commenting on the works of such a scholar.

Rev. James E. Gunther

This monograph presents a challenging springboard for deeper exploration and investigation to member-seminaries of the American Association of Theological Schools. Its implications for church history and Biblical studies stagger my imagination. To think of Moses as an African, to think of Egypt as a part of Africa, open the gates of truth and the opportunity to demythologize Western, North American, theological symbol systems. I recommend it to our laymen and religious educational institutions and Board of Publication.

Rabbi Hailu Paris

Certainly the beginning of Judaeo-Christian-Islamic theology had its origin in the teachings of the indigenous African and Asian peoples of the Nile River, Tigris River, and the Euphrates River valleys. This is just a sample of the background of the origin of the source of the truths all of us preach—The Old and New Testament or Qur'an.

Rev. Sis. Bessie I. Robbinson

I had always wondered what was the true origin of the first Bible, the place where it was written, the people who wrote it, and the name of original. The Lord certainly acts in His mysterious way; would I have expected the answer from other than a member of the clergy? No! Truth has no boundaries. Dr. ben-Jochannan was called to deliver the word and its source of origin. I will have to read the rest of his works.

Additional works available by Dr. Ben

African Origins of the Major Western Religions. 1970*, 1991. 363 pp. (paper $24.95, ISBN 0933121-29-6). First published in 1970, this work continues to be instructive and fresh. Dr. Ben critically examines the history, beliefs, and myths that are the foundation of Judaism, Christianity, and Islam. He highlights the often overlooked African influences and roots of these religions. The Black Classic Press edition is a facsimile edition, with an added index and extended bibliography.

Black Man of the Nile. 1972*, 1989. 381 pp. illus. bibl. (paper $24.95, ISBN 0933121-26-1). In a masterful and unique manner, Dr. Ben uses *Black Man of the Nile* to challenge and expose "Europeanized" African history. He reveals distortion after distortion made in the long record of African contributions to world civilization. Once these distortions are exposed, he attacks them with a vengeance, and provides a spellbinding corrective lesson. Of all the works published by Dr. Ben, this one remains a treasured all-time favorite. Readers continue to demand this work.

Abu Simbel to Ghizeh. 1987*, 1989. 350 pp. illus. gloss. (paper $22.00, ISBN 0933121-27-X). This tour guide is an alternative to guides written for and by Europeans. Dr. Ben draws from his many years of travel, study, and living in Egypt to provide a useful history and guide to ancient Egyptian/African monuments, cultural sites, and prominent people. Although it is intended for readers who plan to travel to Egypt, this guide is helpful to anyone who wants to gain a better understanding of ancient African history.

Africa: Mother of Western Civilization. 1971*, 1988. 750 pp. illus. bibl. (paper $34.95, ISBN 0933121-25-3). Dr. Ben examines the African foundations of Western civilization. In lecture essay format, he identifies and corrects myths about the inferiority and primitiveness of the indigenous African peoples and their descendants. He mentions many authorities on Africa and their works and proves how they are racist in intent. Dr. Ben is often humorous, and always critical of traditional Western scholarship and values.

We The Black Jews. 1983*, 1993. 408 pp. (paper $24.95, ISBN 0933121-40-7). Dr. Ben destroys the myth of a "white Jewish race" and the bigotry that has denied the existence of an African Jewish culture. He establishes the legitimacy of contemporary Black Jewish culture in Africa and the diaspora, and predates its origin before ancient Nile Valley civilizations. This work provides insight and historical relevance to the current discussion of Jewish and Black cultural relationships.

To order, send a check or money order to:

Black Classic Press
P.O. Box 13414
Baltimore, MD 21203-3414

Credit Card Orders Call—1-800-476-8870
Please have your credit card available.

Include $3.00 for the first book ordered, $1.00 for the second,
and .50 cents for each additional title.

* *indicates first year published*